Content Marketing

A Beginner's Guide to Dominating the
Market with Content Marketing

TABLE OF CONTENTS

Free Marketing Blueprint

Marketing can be a complex subject and even after years of experience the same principles still apply.

Give yourself a head start! Grab your free copy of The Marketing Blueprint to help you understand what you need to succeed

To grab your copy of The Marketing Blue Print visit
http://www.mrmarketinghero.com/freebook

Respective authors own all copyrights not held by the publisher.

The information herein is offered for informational purposes solely, and is universal as so. The presentation of the information is without contract or any type of guarantee assurance.

The trademarks that are used are without any consent, and the publication of the trademark is without permission or backing by the trademark owner. All trademarks and brands within this book are for clarifying purposes only and are owned by the owners themselves, not affiliated with this document.

Introduction

I want to thank you and congratulate you for purchasing the book, "Content Marketing: A Beginner's Guide to Dominating the Market with Content Marketing."

This book contains important details on how best to position your business, improve your reputation and brand to attract a wider audience, and realize a rapid business growth.

You will discover that to succeed and effectively dominate your industry, there must be a shift in your mindset and the processes that you utilize to execute your strategies and related tasks. Your foundation must be flexible enough to withstand challenges, yet sturdy enough to maintain the structures and systems that you will implement to construct a profitable and successful business.

We will focus on innovative approaches, tools, and resources that you should utilize in every phase of your content marketing journey. Whether you only have an idea, or you've already started a business, I have highlighted the essential factors that you should consider as you step into the sphere of content marketing and advance as a leader in your respective industry.

Thanks again for purchasing this book. I hope you enjoy it

Chapter 1

What is Content Marketing?

Content is what you use to communicate with your potential customers or existing customers. It includes your pages on your website, your social media channel, blogs, PowerPoint presentations, newsletters, podcasts, and videos.

Though you may be considering all the work you have to do and have started brainstorming, my objective is to keep you focused on what is important. Before we venture on, you must first know what your goal is. Why, you may ask? Because the content should be used as a tool to support your goals. To help you fine-tune your goals, here are some questions to consider: Do you need to develop an email lists? Do you want more viewers to become customers? Do you wish to keep your customers and encourage them to spend more? Once you know what your goals are, you will know if the content you have created is relevant and will meet your objectives.

Content marketing is using "content" to realize your business marketing goal. Content marketing is more than providing information to an audience with the goal of acquiring profits and acquiring a loyal fan base. These are certain factors you must understand:

• You should have a strategic plan in order to be effective. Planning will take time. It is not something that you should do in haste and when you are not focused. Also, you will have to track your goals and evaluate your progress to know when they will need to be modified. You should have various steps outlined that will take you from the first step until you have arrived at your desired target.

• You have to market your content. You cannot create the content, use one medium, and expect the people who use other online resources to know about it just because you have used your preferred medium. You have to showcase your content before an audience.

• Your content must be high-quality and very informative. Do not have the mindset that fluff and "anything goes" can give you mileage. There is so much information at the fingertips of people around the world and they only gravitate to content that is educational, informative, entertaining, and inspirational.

• You must have regular content, not the occasional informational post here and there when you are in the mood to create it. Previously, businesses had the say in what to convey and when to communicate with the public. That has changed as people all over the world have various preferences and various options at the click of a button.

- As already highlighted, your content should help you to achieve your goals.
- When creating content, focus on your specific audience.

Paradigm Shift

You are quite aware what it is like to have conversations with self-centered people. You can pick a neutral topic yet they will always find a way to shine the spotlight on themselves. You can simply be talking about the rainy weather, hoping for conversation, and it will be turned into a monologue. For the talker, it is a wonderful experience. On the other hand, it is not a good experience for the listener.

Similarly, the content that you are creating is not about your business or about you. Your content should not be the opportunity to be self-centered. It is not your brochure or company manual dissected in different parts and you expect the public to be versed on every detail that happened to you and your business. If your audience wants to buy the skin cream that you are advertising, for example, why do you have to mention immaterial and irrelevant details that will not improve their buying experience or make them more informed about the product?

You must realize that the content you are creating is about your audience. You are providing information that will enlighten them, make their lifestyle much easier, eliminate stressful situations in their life, and make them happy and feel like they are connected to a source that adds value to their lives. Your content should be newsworthy, express an opinion about something, offer insights, and be informative.

Differences

Content marketing is not advertising
Content marketing is not advertising, which is a type of structured communication. Advertising focuses on obtaining money quickly. You may turn the pages of a newspaper and see: SALE! SALE! SALE! Buy one get the other ½ price while stock lasts.

With advertising, you are paying a third party to use their medium to capture an audience. In the example given, a business has paid the newspaper an advertising fee to showcase what is being offered. The business will capture the attention of the newspaper's readers. Similarly, it is like going to an event to have an opportunity to see and engage various artists, but you have to pay at the entrance. You do not have access unless you pay.

Content marketing is about producing content to build your own audience. You can use social media, websites, and even pay for advertising, as that is one channel to market your content. However, content marketing is about establishing your own audience.

Think of advertising as waving to someone from across the street and content marketing as not only waving but stopping to engage in conversation and genuinely inquiring how the individual is doing.

Content Marketing is not Public Relations
Public Relations is about the relationship between an organization and the public. There is a difference with PR and Content Marketing also. Content marketing is used daily to engage your audience. PR is usually utilized when there is a special event or negative occasion that needs to be resolved. PR releases are formal and geared around the brand and the message the company wishes to convey to the public. Public relations can be expensive. Content marketing is based on the consumer and can be done in-house, and even if it is outsourced, the costs are affordable. There are parallels, but there is still a distinction.

Content Marketing is not Social Media
Content marketing is about your customers absorbing the knowledge you create, whereas social media is more about sharing that knowledge. Social media is used to distribute your content.

Advertising, Public Relations and Social Media are the promotional avenues that you can use to market your content. However, note the differences so you can create an effective content marketing strategy.

Chapter 2

The Importance of Consistent and High-Quality Content

Long ago, you had to be in a library or educational facility to obtain specific information. Later on, you had to have a computer and the internet to have access to certain information. Today, with just one click of a button on a phone or other mobile device, anyone can access information that used to only be housed in encyclopedias and library reference books.

We do not have to be stationary at the computer to surf the internet. We can check and read material whenever and wherever we may go. With so much information available to people around the world, you have to ensure that the content you produce is more valuable than that of your competitors.

Brand Awareness
The members of your audience have their own habits. Perhaps they have been loyal to your competitors. However, with your content you can get them to change their habits in alignment with your goals. Having quality content strategically positions your brand before an audience. The more they see your brand, the more they can recognize it.

Have you ever walked or driven along a certain route for months or even years, then one day someone points something out to you, which you had never seen before? Then all of a sudden you to start to spot the same thing in various places and enjoy it, when before it was non-existent to you. Or have you ever been introduced to someone and thereafter you spot the individual very frequently? It is the same thing with brand awareness.

Creating content will ensure that your audience has something to talk about. When people include your business in their conversation, they teach and inform other people who may not have been aware of your brand or about your product or service.

Content Marketing Makes You a Reliable and Authoritative Source
The more regularly you create quality content, the more you will be viewed as a reliable and credible source. It is not about quantity. It is not about how much you produce, but what you have produced that can distinguish you from your competitors.

Your audience will grow to respect and highly regard your work.

It Captures Audience Attention
Have you ever been offered a sample of a food item that is so tasty that you not only take a second helping but you want to know about the chef? It is the same way when you have quality content. The more remarkable your content, the more you will have people returning to read, see, or hear what you have created.

Increase in Traffic
The more powerful content you create, the more it will enhance your website traffic and search engine optimization (SEO).
Search engine optimization is a way to obtain traffic from search results. Webpages and content on your pages are displayed and ranked according to what the search engines find to be appropriate. For example, if a tourist stops you in the street and asks you to tell him the best place to get a meal, preferably something cheap and in walking distance, you won't send him to a fancy upscale restaurant in a far and remote location. Likewise, if someone looks for a specific topic in search engines, he or she will be given a list of information that is more relevant. The better your content, the more highly it will be ranked and noticed by viewers.

Website Terms and Information

Links

An inbound link refers to a hyperlink that is on another site and leads back to you. An inbound link is sometimes called a backlink.

For example, if you are having an event, you will advertise it in your business place. You may also ask businesses to advertise your event and they may give out flyers to their customers. Individuals reading the flyer will know that you exist and will know more about your business. If this was online, then the business will provide links to your website so people can click the link and be directed to your website.

When you have a lot of inbound links, search engines will rank your page higher on the list. Inbound links is referred to as off-page search engine optimization.

On-page search engine optimization involves positioning keywords within your headlines, subheadings, tags, body content and links. Use a main keyword for each page. Do not use many keywords. Insert your keywords in your headings and subheadings. Also, place them in the content of your body, but don't overdo it.

Bear in mind that though you wish to rank well in the search engines, you are writing for your audience. Thus, ensure that you strike an appropriate balance. Your audience is your first priority.

Meta tag

Meta tag is a code used for search engines to ascertain what your site is about. Most websites have a management system for you to edit meta tags without you having to be an expert in coding, so don't worry. With the advancement of technology, resources are provided for you to make your work much easier. However, you should know what a meta tag is. The objective of the meta tag is to describe your web page for the systems that collect web data. You may have seen it but do not know what it is. Let us assume that a website is called Marketing Software. It may look something like this for a title:

<title>Marketing Software</title>

The description may look like this:

<meta name= "Description" content= "be more engaging, be more appealing.. Marketing Software...">

This is just the code for the system. You do not need to be versed in coding for you to be a great content marketer. It is listed here because perhaps you have seen things that look like this, but you weren't sure about the relevance.

The good news is that many of the resources that allow you to build your site using their platform already have the settings in place. If you are unsure, you can consult with a programmer or website developer.

Redirect your page when necessary

If your website address has changed, make sure that you redirect your page to the right place. For example, if your website was www.example.com and you have changed your address to www.goodexample.com, do what is necessary to redirect your page. When visitors go to www.example.com they will see a message "Page Not Found." They may automatically assume that your business no longer exists, and that means you just lost some potential customers. Therefore, make sure to redirect your page. Your hosting company and the place where you bought your domain will be able to provide information on how to direct your page.

The Do's and Don'ts

Content Creation

General Information
Do ensure that you have a specific objective for the content you create. What do you want your audience to do after reading your content? Are you building your email lists? Do you want them to sign up for something?

Do not use more words than necessary. Focus more on the message. You can also use images to assist with conveying your message.

Do know who your audience is.

Do not use uncommon words that leave your audience clueless. Imagine for a second that you are a scientist and regularly give lectures to scholars and academics. You also have a blog where you talk about gardening. Your content should be completely distinct so that anyone wanting to know about gardening can follow, as opposed to having to use a dictionary to understand the scientific terms you have used.

Web Content Writing Information
If you spot an error on your website, change it immediately.

Do remove your tweets if they have errors.

Ensure that your Facebook page is presentable, once you are using it for marketing purposes. Yes, you can keep it interactive, but ensure that it is devoid of blurred pictures and errors.

Do avoid long paragraphs. Writing on the web is different than print. The attention span for viewers online is shorter than those who opt to read printed material. Therefore, keep your paragraphs short.

If you are unsure of anything, the answer is a click away, so research it. It is better to take the time to do so rather than have errors in your work.

Editing and Grammar

Ensure that you give yourself a break before editing your work. The longer break you have, you will be able to spot the errors quicker when you return to your work. You do not always spot errors while writing. It is when your mind is refreshed that you see things more clearly.

Carefully, read each sentence at a time. Do not speed read, but instead take your time.

Observe what patterns you may have and look to spot them. What are your trouble spots? Do you always confuse their and there? Every time you see these words, take your time to ensure that you have used them correctly.

Change what needs correcting when you spot it, whether it is the structure of a sentence, punctuation, or spelling.

Ensure that you read the entire work at a reasonable speed. Do not rush when checking for errors.

Storytelling Tips
Tell stories that you pique your interest
Sometimes we fall in the trap of trying to convey a story we heard, but it is not communicated with the passion and gusto of the original storyteller. When you retell it, it may sound dull and boring. You may wonder if you have the skill to tell stories. Yes, you do. The key is to tell something that you are passionate about and not what someone else finds interesting.

Make time and prepare
Preparation is very important when telling stories. Do the proper research and make sure that you have enough information to enhance what you wish to communicate.

Remove insignificant parts

If bits and pieces of your story are irrelevant and drag your story to a halt, instead of merrily moving along, remove it. Determine if you really need that bit of information. If you don't need it, take it out.

Listening Formats

All of the information above applies. If you are speaking, bear these in mind also for your listeners.

Have self-assurance

If you are using audio, podcasts, webinars, and similar formats to tell your story, tell your story with confidence. If you are unsure of what you are conveying and doubtful, it will affect how your listeners view you and digest the information.

Pace yourself

Do not hurry along. Speak slowly and clearly so your listeners can hear you.

Visual

If you are using video content, engage your audience by using eye-contact.

Writing style and voice

Voice

Voice is a way of writing that distinguishes you from other writers. When you call a friend and simply say, "Hello," your friend can detect your voice without you having to identify yourself. It is the same way that your readers can identify you. Though they cannot "hear" you from reading your work, they can read your content and identify with your personality. Perhaps your writing is laced with humor or a touch sarcasm or you are very compassionate. Whatever it may be, your voice is what sets you apart from other writers.

Style
Your style is broader and goes beyond your personality. Let us imagine for a second that you are in line at the supermarket. A friend is behind you, cannot see your face but calls your name confidently and is sure that it is you in the line. Your friend may tell you she identified you by your style. Perhaps you always wear a unique set of earrings, or your hair is styled in a fashionable way or you are flamboyant in your dressing or you like wearing baseball caps. In the same way, a reader can identify you by your style. One way to identify style might be your sentence structure. Are your sentences long and do they meander across the page to get to the final destination? Or are they short and chirpy? Are your sentences packed with many metaphors and imagery so your readers feel that they were right there with you, seeing exactly what you saw?

Right and wrong pertains to grammar. Style is not a matter of what is right or wrong, but what uniquely is your way of writing.

There are four main writing categories and everyone has a specific style.

1. Expository

In this category, a writer informs the readers about a particular topic or subject. It requires facts and supporting information. It is commonly used in textbooks and this type of writing is logical, organized, and straightforward.

2. Descriptive

The focus is more on describing a character, an event, or a place. The objective is more to entertain the audience with the beauty of words. More adverbs, imagery, figurative language, and adjectives are used in this form of writing.

3. Persuasive

The writer gives reasons and justifies his point of view to convince the reader. Sometimes, things are exaggerated and can even be very dramatic to emotionally influence an audience.

4. Narrative

The writer narrates the story. Depending on the genre, a particular type of sentence structure will be used to build excitement or suspense.

Social Media Writing

Avoid your formal voice

There is a difference when communicating on social media platforms. Social media is not as formal as other forms of communication. It's like socializing, letting your hair down, relaxing your shoulders. Therefore, you have to use your casual voice whether or not you are an executive wearing a business suit.

When you start a conversation with someone, do you use a serious face and sound like you are a politician speaking to government officials? Of course not. Try not to sound like you are at a business convention when using social media.

You should ask questions of those you are communicating with and avoid sounding as if you are in the boardroom. Your social voice should be warm and engaging as if you are talking to a friend.

It doesn't mean that you will break all the grammar rules by using question marks when you should use full stops and abandoning all that you know. Just keep it casual.

Short and simple is better
Social media is not a place to sound like a lecturer giving an academic talk. Do not have 40 paragraphs of text where your audience has to scroll and scroll and scroll and scroll to read what you wish to convey. You can condense your summary if you wish, but keep your longer content for other forums. If you don't, you will lose the interest of your audience. Think about it. When you go to a place to hang out and unwind, do you want to keep talking about the latest business policies and talk in detail about everything that happened on the job and sound as if you have read the company's manual? Or do you inquire about what your friends are doing and keep the conversation entertaining?

If you do have a long form of content, provide the link to where individuals can read it and if you do provide commentary, keep it short. Twitter has 140 characters, so there is a limit on how much you can convey.

Action words

Social media is for socializing, but it doesn't mean that you should forget your business goals and objectives. Encourage your followers to perform some kind of action. Do you want them to click on the link? Do you want them to read the post on your blog and share their views? Is there a video you want them to watch on YouTube?

Personal language

Include the right pronouns. Do not speak in the third person and sound formal. For example, if you are the owner of business called We Deliver, do not post, "The owner of We Deliver would like to inform the customers..." You can simply say, "I would like to share some exciting news with you..." When you use the pronouns "you" and "I," it sounds more engaging. Write as if you are speaking to one person.

Have fun with punctuation

As said above, although you are on social media, you should not break all the grammatical rules. However, you can still have fun with your communication. You are not writing for a group of business consultants. You are free to capitalize words for emphasis and use more than one exclamation point. For example, you can say, "I have GREAT news!!" You will surely have your followers curious.

Edit

Review your work. You do not want your words to be misconstrued. You can have a friend or associate read your post before you post it. For example, you may have wanted to say, "Do visit We Deliver for all your delivery needs," but in reality, you posted, "Do not visit We Deliver for all your delivery needs." One word can be detrimental.

Tips for writing interesting headlines
• Use numbers
• Include interesting adjectives
• Include words such as What, Why, How and When
• Include an incredible promise. Make sure you fulfill it, though. You want to capture your readers' attention not jeopardize your credibility by making promises you cannot keep.

Using humor

Who does not like to laugh? We all do. One injection of humor can surely brighten anyone's day. Use humor, but don't overdo it. Do not share jokes at the expense of a group of people. It may be funny to you, but it may be misconstrued differently. Save the raunchy jokes for your friends and family and remember the goals of your business. You want to make people laugh, not view you in a negative light.

Topics to write about

The content that you provide must have value to your readers. Here are some examples of what you can write about.

- Offer an analysis of an article on the market
- Provide case studies
- Answer questions that you have received
- Mention dialogue that you've had on social media
- Interviews
- Topics in the news.

Chapter 3

Know Your Audience

Persona Profile

You have to know who you are conveying your message to. You have to create a persona profile, which is a profile of your ideal buyer. Identify important factors about the members of your audience.

These are some questions to assist you:

What are your members' demographics?
What are the facts about your audience? What is the age, gender, and location? If you are already in business with data analytics, you can analyze data from your database or management software system. If you have not set one up as yet, list the key factors of your ideal profile.

What are their decision points?
What would make your audience consider your content? What problem or dilemma or need do they have that would make

them consider your source? Do you have a viable solution to their needs and can you help them resolve their problems or point them to resources which they can use?

What are their responsibilities?

You would not know about their individual responsibilities. The responsibilities I am referring to are general responsibilities. Are your customers on a tight budget? Let us imagine, for example, that you provide information on how to stretch a dollar and how to shop for deals. You should in no way expect to think that your audience comprises of millionaires and billionaires. If you want to cater to millionaires and billionaires, then readjust your business goals and change your content accordingly.

What are the characteristics of the members of your audience? Do they buy fancy cars and private jets, or do they camp out on weekends and enjoy nature? What are their attitudes and opinions?

Content briefs

You will have to create what is known as an editorial brief or content brief. These are the points you must consider when planning your brief.
Fundamentals

- What are your objectives?

Why are you doing this? Is it for popularity or to earn a profit? Do you want to help people or do you want people to know more about your brand? Or both?

•   Who are you targeting?

You would have already answered this in your persona profile.

•   What key points do you want people to digest?

When you buy medication from the pharmacy, you listen to what is said. If you have to take your medication with food, that will the foremost thing on your mind. You won't take them randomly or on an empty stomach because you have forgotten the instructions. Similarly, what do you want your audience to have on their minds while reading your content? What do you want them to remember?

•   What supporting evidence do you have?

If you are informing people about the latest technological device, why should your audience believe you? Have you tried it for yourself? If you offer information about real estate, do you know much about the topic? This is very important, as you want your readers to see you as an authority on the topic and value what you have to say. Therefore, provide supporting evidence.

•   What is the tone of voice you will be using?

Funny? Witty? Compassionate? There are many options, but you have to know what will be best for you.

•   Execution

To implement your content marketing plan, what budget do you need? What is your timing? Do you have guidelines? What format will you use?

Building on the Fundamentals

Be Confident

Just because you are new to content marketing doesn't mean that you should approach your work with uncertainty. Neither does being confident mean that you should overlook the rules because you think you know everything and you are a magnet for attracting an audience. Being confident means that you are aiming to achieve the most you can achieve with the tools before you. It is a mindset. Once you have the correct mindset, it will reflect in what you do and what you produce.

If you will be working with a group of people to provide your content, inform the group what you aspire to achieve, and also inject that level of confidence within your team members.

Beyond Demographics

What beliefs and behavioral patterns, biases, and dislikes are held by the consumers that you are catering to? Your demographics will show you the age and location, for example, but what about the beliefs of your audience? What causes them to buy? This information is termed "psychographics."

To help you gain a better understanding, if you already have a business, you can conduct interviews with your customers. Include those who may be categorized as your worst customer and also your best customer. You will better understand how your business is viewed by your audience and also what interests them.

Another way to examine this is by using your data. For example, let us imagine that you have a website with health content. You had free giveaways for your topic on diabetes and also on cholesterol. When you check your data, the number of people who opted for the free giveaway about the diabetes topic was three times the number of those who downloaded information on cholesterol. From what the report is showing you, you will realize that more members of your audience are concerned about diabetes or want to know more about it.

If you want to know more, you can also offer surveys on your website for people to give honest feedback. The results can provide you with a better insight as to why your audience will buy a product or gravitate toward a product more than something else.

What do you want your audience to consider?
What do you want your audience to feel after reading your content? If you are producing information on health, do you want them to feel overwhelmed and that they allowed their life to get out of control? Do you reprimand them for overeating and not exercising? Are you condescending in you tone? Was that your intention, or do you want your audience to feel that it is never too late to begin? Do you want them to feel empowered and that they can do everything that they have set their minds to achieve and you will help them along the way?

Once you have a better understanding of what you wish to achieve, your content will reflect it.

Tell a Story

Outline what angle you will take your story. Don't just create, but strategize what angle is best to achieve your goals. For example, if you owned a health website, you can tell your story about what caused you to start the website. What challenges did you have? What was your wake-up call? How did you achieve your health goals? Your audience will connect with you more knowing that you once struggled and are now triumphant.

Content Producers
You have identified your audience, you have your content brief, what is your next move? It is time to produce your content. You do not have to wait until the end to think about it. However, it is placed here because sometimes when you have already earmarked someone for the job, when you have formalized your strategy, you may realize that the person is not best suited for the role.

For example, in your content brief you may have adjusted a few things and have decided that the end product will focus on fashion designs. Imagine that you have already identified a writer whose specialty is in sports. The content that is produced has more to deal with what athletes are wearing when competing. On the other hand, you were more interested in the latest designs coming out of Europe and what the highly paid models are wearing.

Whereas you were hoping to attract a fashion-conscious audience, because of the content produced by the content producer, you have attracted sports fans. Perhaps that may have been your initial intention, but during the brief you adjusted a few things. It is very important that you know what you hope to achieve and what stepping stones will take you there. That way you can inform the people who will help you with your content so everyone has the same mindset.

Who do you have in mind to write your content or assist you with creating your content? Or do you plan to do everything yourself? It all depends on what your business objectives are. You cannot look at what your competitor is doing, for your competitor's goals would be completely different from yours even though you may be producing the same thing.

Your foundation must be strong, so select your team with care. You can select an agency or hire freelancers to assist you with your content.

Hiring
When hiring, you will have certain qualities and skills that you are looking for. You should look at someone who is enthusiastic and talented rather than someone who is just writing because "it is just a job." What does the person like about writing?

Does the person know about content marketing and have any ancillary skills? Does the person keep deadlines? Does the writer have the ability to multitask?

You can also inquire how the writer determines what topics to write about and what format they would take. This question will give you more insight into the person's thought process and what motivates his or her action. Or perhaps the writer uses data and analytics and recent trends to decide what topic to write on. You would hire someone who can offer suggestions and advice.

Editorial Calendar
Your next step is to organize your priorities. What will you be publishing and when will it be published? Do not take this step for granted. You surely insert your personal events on a calendar as a reminder. Likewise, you have to schedule when you will create your content and what supporting activities are needed to do so.

Do not produce content just for the sake of feeling like you are doing something. Stick to your plan to keep your focus.

Places to Publish Your Content
Your website is where you will start. Think of it as your home base. Then you will distribute your content through various channels including email, YouTube, Twitter, Facebook, LinkedIn and the host of other platforms that are available at your fingertips. Only you can decide what platforms are best for you. However, be open to trying new things and exploring various options.

Content marketing does not involve scrambling to find an audience and then building your content to cater to them. Content marketing is strategic and anything that is well thought out will take time. Building the foundation is not something that can rushed. Once you have invested in content and it is worthy and valuable, the audience will be attracted to your platform.

Chapter 4

Blogging

"Blog" is the shortened name for "web log." It is a log of entries on a website. It can be one where different people are contributors or a blog can be written solely by the owner of the website.

As a blogger, you should be passionate about the topics you choose. If you are enthusiastic about what you doing, it will reflect in your content. The content on your blog is owned by you. You set the rules, unlike other social media platforms where you have to abide by their rules. You can build your audience via social sharing and offering an opportunity to comment.

To ensure that your blog is aligned with your objectives, these are some steps to consider.

Domain Name
If you do not have a website at this point in time, you should consider a domain name. It is the first point of contact with the

public. When choosing a domain name, ensure that it is easy to remember and spell. A website with a name that is hard to pronounce and even harder to spell is not something anyone wants to be bothered with. You can use one of your keywords in your domain name if you unsure of what to use. For example, let us assume you have a business and wish to talk about the various types of fans on the market and there is a brand called Wer which is a brand that is relatively new on the market. However, you like the design. You wish to come up with a name. If viewers see a site thebestfans.com or wer.com, they wouldn't have to wonder what the "thebestfans" site is all about as you have used your keyword "fan" in the domain name.

Hosting and Themes

You have to decide who will host your domain name. Therefore, do your research and see which company's rates are affordable and what they have to offer. Also, decide which platform you will use for your blog. Whose design will you use? There are various sites that offer themes for bloggers, such as WordPress. Decide which one is best for you. If you will use a free theme regardless of which site you will use, ensure that the background, header images, and custom menus are presentable. Make sure you can also have proper data analytics so you can check your data in the future.

The worst possible thing you can do is to have a beautiful blog with all the eye-catching details, but there is no feature for you to access your data. Remember that content marketing is more than eye-catching content. You have to strategize to achieve your goals. Make sure that the blog host has all the necessary resources for you to realize your goal.

You also have the option of paying for premium themes with your respective design company of choice. Make your selection carefully if you do opt for this method rather than using the free themes. If you are paying for something, make sure that you know what you will receive in exchange.

Logo

Do you have a logo? If you don't, you should get one as it helps people with identifying your brand immediately. When hiring a designer, ensure that you convey the correct information about your goals and business objectives. You can ask your friends and family members for suggestions if you are unsure of whether the logo you have chosen conveys the right message. You can also run a competition where various designers create logos and then choose the best one.

Plugins

A plugin is a type of software that gives your website more functionality. There are various plugins for WordPress, and by using them you can add more features to your website. For example, email clients may use a software to encrypt email. One plugin that you are familiar with, is Adobe Flash Player. Sometimes when you go on various websites, you may see a message alerting you that Flash Player needs to be installed or updated.

The Flash Player plugin allows you to see content in a format that will give you a better experience. For example, if you click on a video, you will want to see the video from beginning to end with no complications rather than reloading it every couple of seconds because it keeps stopping. If you are obtaining your plugins from various third party developers, be careful with what you use on your website. How well they operate depends on how well they were developed in the first place. If you are not sure about this leg of the journey, consult someone who knows about websites and plugins.

Writing
What you write about depends on your business objectives. We have already discussed the essentials of writing for your audience. Remember that blogging is one way to strategize. It is not the only way.

Perhaps you may wonder why you should blog. These are reasons why you should embrace it.

A blog improves your search optimization.
Once you are operating from your own domain and not a third party blogging website, by using your keywords and providing links to other web content, you can improve how well your audience finds you when doing a search. Using the example above, if someone wants to know about what brands of fans are popular choices and they do their research in the search engines, the websites that offer reviews and suggestions will appear. Let us assume that the blogger on the best fans has two years of solid and valuable content with many comments and

feedback, so the website will be listed higher in the search engines.

On the other hand, if the domain name is not as strong as it could be, you are using a third-party platform site like www.wer/thirdpartyplatform.com and the site only contains pictures of fans and a brief overview, your ranking will not be as high as the other option where the owner has been continuously blogging about fans.

The blog belongs to you.
Let us examine this scenario. Your name is Nate Myers and you are a photographer. You own a Facebook page where you post adorable photos. Your followers know how to contact you. Since opening your Facebook page, you have seen a steady growth of clients. You are running a contest, many people are taking part, and you will announce the winner in five hours.

All is well...until Facebook shuts down your page for violating one of the company's terms and policies. The last thing you posted was a picture of two adorable puppies playing with a ball and you wonder what in the picture was in violation. You search the photo for clues, yet you cannot figure out what you have done to cause your page to be in question. You contact Facebook contesting the company's claims. Two days later, you reclaim your page with angry followers upset that you didn't post who won the contest. They are asking if you were scamming them. You have to appease them and find a way to salvage your reputation.

It was after contacting Facebook that you realized there was a mix up. Someone in a different country reported you, but the person made an error. The violator was Nate Mayers. The complainer made a typo and it read Nate Myers. You finally receive the wakeup call that although you have a Facebook account, you are at the whim and mercy of the company's policies and someone else's mistake. Your account can be hacked or shut down at any time, and there is nothing you can do until it is resolved. On the other hand, the content on your blog is owned by you. With your own blog, you do not have to wonder if you will be locked out of your account.

Blogs are a 24-hour source of communication.
You can publish your content at any time when you own a blog. Using the example of being locked out of your Facebook account, during that time you could not communicate with your audience. By having a blog, people from anywhere in the world can view your blog and see who won the contest, rather than wonder what happened when they didn't hear from you.

You can use any format on your blog.
You can use text, videos, charts, PDFs, e-books, whitepapers, audio, PowerPoint presentations, and any other format on your blog. You are not limited. If there are any limitations, it is because your blog was not properly designed to incorporate certain formats. That is why you must ensure that your blog is properly designed and hosted.

A blog is easy to use.

Anyone can own a blog and be successful once they follow certain guidelines as listed above. You do not need to know about computer programming, nor do you have to be versed in the various forms of software.

A blog is affordable.
Having a blog is very affordable. You do not have to worry about taking a loan to own one.

There are other things to consider if you decide to blog. Here are a few of them:

Administrator
If you are not working alone and you have other contributors, you can determine who you want to be your blog administrator. This person will be responsible for the overall management of the blog. The individual has to market the blog through various avenues on social media platforms, develop the plan, select the target keywords, and know about the latest search engine optimization topics.

Blog Guideline
What is the word length of your posts? Does your blog contribute toward your business goal? What tone will you use? In your blog guidelines, you should answer these questions so when you sit to write, you keep focused instead of wondering what the next step is. Publication Schedule

You may have the date of publication marked on your editorial calendar, but what about the activities that lead up to the publication date? Having a publication schedule allows you to track your progress. Who will be contributing to your blog? When will the person or persons send you the information? Who will edit what was written? Are there pictures or videos to complement the article? Will you contact a photographer or will you ask your friend who told you she has a lovely picture for your post? Did you send your friend a reminder to look for the picture? Your publication schedule allows you to organize and plan the process.

Give Credit

Though the site belongs to you, if you have other bloggers, give them credit when it is due. You can create a profile of your bloggers with pictures and bios so your audience knows who they are interacting with. If you do not wish to take that route, make sure that your bloggers know that they are appreciated.

After you have written your post...

Check for keywords.

Examine your content and select the topics in your post. Use keyword tools to observe popular terms and phrasing. For example, you can use Google Trends. It shows the frequency that a search term is entered in the search engine. Based on what you have observed, modify your content accordingly. This can be your content, title, or meta tags.

RSS feed

RSS stands for Rich Site Summary and it is a system for providing frequent web content. It allows anyone who utilizes it to stay up to date on information. It allows anyone to obtain the latest content from your website. If your regular bakery provides your favorite cookies once a week and then they sell them twice a week, you would want to know about it. The bakery may display a sign or have flyers so customers know about it. Likewise, an RSS feed allows an audience to know about updated changes on a website.

Once you have enabled the correct settings on your website, when you publish a post, it is automatically updated to your social networking sites that you are connected with. So rather than publishing on your blog, then signing into Facebook to post, then signing in to other social sites to post, all you need to do is publish once and let the software do the rest.

Look for other related blog posts.
By commenting on other blogs, you can generate traffic to your site, too. Do not be obvious. Remember your content is for adding value to an audience; it's not a sales pitch. Don't comment on someone's blog, "Hi guys, check out my post at thebestfans.com. I have what you are looking for so just click the link below!!!" Can you imagine posting that on a blog that deals with recipes? If you do, do not be surprised if your comment is deleted or the followers of that blog refer to you as behaving out of line. The aim is to attract an audience, so be mindful of what you do.

Share your post with your target audience.
Share the information with the people who will be interested in your content. Earlier I addressed the demographics and

psychographics. Moreover, if you did surveys and questionnaires, you will have more insight on what your audience members are thinking and doing.

Feature your posts in your newsletter.
If you have a newsletter or are thinking of getting one, and you are worried about where to find content, your problem will be solved once you a blogger. You can incorporate headlines and a few sentences to inform your subscribers about the topics on your site.

Have other writers comment your blog post.
Rather than commenting, "Hi guys, check out my post at thebestfans.com. I have what you are looking for so just click the link below," you will gain more mileage if a blogger mentions your post. Let's assume a recipe blogger spent an hour preparing tasty treats. In her post, she comments, "While the cakes were in the oven I took a break and enjoyed the breeze from my x fan. My kitchen is always hot, but thanks to The Best Fans blog, I was able to buy mine at a discount." Readers will want to know about your blog and what discounts you have to offer. Simply ask several bloggers to mention your post and ensure that you make the right selection. For example, if someone's blog is littered with discriminatory topics and your blog is about equal rights, but you are adamant that the person may want to feature your blog, do not be surprised if when you ask, the blogger wants nothing to do with your blog on justice for all. Be realistic and choose wisely.

Dealing with Trolls

Have you ever enjoyed an article online so much that you scanned the comments, smiling until you read the most insulting comments that totally distract other readers and commenters from the topic? You are only a reader. Can you imagine how the publisher of the content must feel? There are people who have made it their purpose to offend and upset as much as they can on the internet. These people are referred to as trolls.

They initiate arguments, post comments to incite, provoke readers, and go off topic. It is harassment online. Their objective is to disrupt. Some individuals view their comments as sincere and valid contributions. Nonetheless, when you publish content, you will attract individuals who are malicious in their postings.

They hide behind the anonymity of the internet and most of the time they use fake usernames.

In the United Kingdom, the Malicious Communications Act 1988 and the Communications Act 2003 addresses this subject matter. Individuals have been imprisoned in the United Kingdom for online harassment.

So how do you deal with trolls?

• You should have a policy on your website and other platforms outlining what type of comments are allowed and those that will not be tolerated.

• Completely ignore them. Trolls vie for attention. Their goal is to get you mad and upset. Do not give in. Do not get angry and lash out at them, for then they have accomplished what they set out to do in the first place.

• Another option is to respond in a lighthearted way. I'm sure in real life, you have smiled at people who have offended you when in fact you feel like screaming. Use experience to withstand the taunting and teasing.

• Take away their power. You do not have to name them and let the world know their identity, but you can find ways to make what they have said insignificant.

• Delete the comments if you have the power to do so. Most websites usually allow you to approve of comments before they are published to the world. When you go through the comments and they are rude and littered with profanity, just delete them.

• You can also ban members if they are known for their disruptive tendencies.

• You can prevent an audience from commenting. The disadvantage with this option is that while you are disabling one person or a few persons, you are stifling great discussion and dialogue on your blog with the rest of the world. So if you do use this option, be mindful of the long-term effect.

• If you do not have the time, you can hire people to monitor your content when published. So rather than waiting 12 hours later when you actually have the time to check, someone will be able to remove distasteful comments as soon as they appear.

• A community of loyal supporters can take care of trolls without you having to do so. However, they need to be mature and experienced at handling trolls. You do not want your comment feed to be littered with a back and forth series of insults between your loyal supporters and trolls.

• Take the comments into consideration. Sometimes the comments can genuinely be coming from a customer who has had a bad experience. Take the time to read and ascertain whether the comment is valid enough for you to take action.

• Respond with facts. When trolls are spreading wrong information and rumors, rather than wait for the rumors to die, you should answer with the facts right away. You should not want anything controversial hampering the credibility of your product or service.

• If a mistake is highlighted by a troll, make the correction and you can admit that you were wrong. You can inform the person that you have made the corrections.

Chapter 5

What You Should Not Overlook

Avoid using the third person

Do you remember that one teacher in high school that no matter how interesting a topic was, they made it boring with their tone? It was enough to make you fall asleep. There are also fond memories of those teachers who can take any topic and make it so entertaining that you were sorry when the class was over. It had to do with their teaching style.

Similarly, ensure that your writing style is like your favorite teacher's approach to imparting knowledge to students. You may not realize it, but using the third person is perceived by your audience as very formal and uninteresting.

Imagine there are two companies who were awarded for their sterling contribution for their fund-raising activities in the community. You read this on one website: Wildflower Corporation was honored at the mayor's gala. Then you go to another website and see this: Hooray! Guess what? We received an award at the mayor's gala just a few hours ago and we couldn't have done it without your support. Thank you!

The first one sounds very detached, as if the company is reporting about another company instead of its own. Do not be robotic while writing.

Do not neglect to use visuals.
Pictures, videos, and PowerPoint presentations can all be used to convey your message. Your content will be more appealing, so use them.

Know the profile of your audience.
Do not downplay your demographics and psychographics. Do not pay the least attention to your personal profile and related activities.

Share your content.
Do not focus so much on blogging that you overlook other platforms where you can place your content. Content marketing is more than blogging. Blogging is a channel to distribute your content. Do not, however, focus 99% of your time on blogging and 1% on other forums.

When you do blog, remember to share what you have written. Sharing is more than spending five seconds to post it in a forum. You have to strategically think of where you will share your content. What are your goals? What do you want? Where is your audience? For example, if your website is based on gardening resources and there are various gardening groups on Facebook, sign up and share your information. Sharing your content with a Facebook group that is more interested in fashion will not give you your desired outcome. Therefore, plan properly.

40 Questions and Answers

1.   Is your headline straightforward and on target?
If your headline is more than 55 characters, you stand the chance of it being chopped off on the search results in Google. You have to be creative in crafting your headline. Will your audience know what you are conveying, or do they have to read the entire article to understand your message? If people are unsure before they click on a link, they will move right along to another page or platform.

2.   Is your topic something that someone will type in the search engines?
For example, let's assume you wrote an article on how to get over a hangover quickly, and you post it around the holidays. It is a topic people will want to know more about as around the festive season people overindulge. On the other hand, if you wrote an article where you reminisce about Easter in the middle of the Christmas Holidays, you will not get as many hits as topics that are relevant to Christmas and the New Year.

3.   Is your headline interesting?
Does your headline make your audience want to click immediately? Do you have popular keywords and phrases in your headline? If your headline is not as interesting as it can be, it will not rank significantly well in Google and other search engines.

4.   Is the introduction of your blog engaging?
If your readers are hooked in the middle of the blog instead from the beginning, you will have to consider rewording your introduction or shifting your paragraph. Not everyone will read on, and you will lose a significant amount of readers if they find your introduction dull. Make sure that your introduction piques their curiosity and makes them want to read more.

5.   Is the body of your content short and sweet or longwinded?
To delve into the body of your content, make sure that there are few paragraphs between the introduction and the body of content. If the reader is only digesting the meat of your content after ten long paragraphs, then you have surely missed the mark. Therefore, condense, reword, and restructure.

6.   Did you include any visuals in your blog post?
You can never go wrong by including a picture or video in your blog post. We are in the era where people expect to see pictures and videos. If your blog post is just text, some of your readers may click over to another website that provides visuals. Think of it this way—if a friend tells you about her wonderful vacation and the beautiful scenery at the destination, would you want to see the pictures as well, or is hearing the details enough?

7.   Does your content have subheadings?
It is your preference whether you want to use subheadings or not. However, remember that the content is for the audience

and not for you. Subheadings make it easier for readers to navigate their way through your article.

8. Are you using the correct amount of lines for a paragraph on the blog?

Remember it is not a book you are writing, a manual, whitepaper, or magazine. Six lines is acceptable. If you do opt to use more lines, keep your sentences short.

9. Is your tone conversational?

Use "you" and "I" in your content to make it more personal and conversational.

10. What other way can you make your content conversational?

You can italicize your questions. It gives an appearance that you are more personable.

11. Are you making your content more attractive?

You should use any tool that will enhance your content. Examples of useful tools includes audio, video, charts, and images.

12. Is your content filled with substance or fluff?

You do know what it is like to buy that bag of your favorite potato chip. You open it and the air escapes and you are left with ¼ of what you initially thought was in the bag. Don't you feel absolutely cheated? In the same way, you should not have content that is full of fluff. As was emphasized from the beginning, create content that is of value.

13.   Are you using the correct vocabulary?

Do readers have to have a dictionary close by to read your content? Do they also need to reference an encyclopedia to understand certain terms? Do not use words that will cause you to lose your audience. Make sure that the people you have hired to write your content are experienced enough to know the right wording for your audience.

14.   Is your post formatted properly?

Did you use bulleted points and other features properly? Make the reading experience easier for your audience. Take the time to format your content correctly.

15.   Did you include authority figures in your blog post?

You should include quotes from the experts to make your content more reliable. If, for example, your content is predominantly about diabetes, where did you source your information? Did you quote what doctors and experts have said?

16.   Did you provide supporting facts?

If you make a claim, it is always best to provide facts to support your claim. You can use charts and statistics and similar resources. The last thing you would want is in the middle of reading your post, someone leaves your website to open a browser to find proof of what you have claimed. In the interim, the reader may forget to return to your post as his or her interest has shifted.

17.   At the end of your blog post, do you have a summary?
A nice summary should be 150 words or 200, if you need extra words. If your summary is 500 words, then it may be construed as rambling. If you find you have a lot to say in the summary, you need to restructure your post. Perhaps you need to include another paragraph and not pack everything in the summary.

18.   Do you have a way to collect emails?
You should have a system in place to obtain your audience emails. You can incorporate a lead magnet which is something that persuades people to sign up. For example, you can offer something for free, once they sign up.

19.   Is it really that important to share content on other platforms when I have a blog?
Yes. A blog is but one way to share your content. Perhaps you are not really a sociable person and haven't quite gotten the hand of other platforms. You can hire someone to assist you just as you have other people to help you with your content. How will people find you if they do not know about you? Blogging is one way, but not the only way, to share your information.

20.   Does your post have social sharing buttons?
You should have social sharing buttons so that your audience can also share the content with their friends and associates. There is nothing wrong with asking your audience to share what you have published.

21.   Did you use expert sources in your sharing platform?

You should mention your sources for others to share. I am not referring to just in your content but in the format where others can share. For example, you can tweet, "Eating more of x lowers your cholesterol." You may give your food item and set it up so others can retweet it. Let's suppose that in your research, you discovered that Jim Jones, a celebrity, ate the same food item and it improved his health. Jim Jones now has his own show and radio broadcast advocating for the use of the food item. Doctors have confirmed what Jim Jones is saying is correct. One of the doctors is highly respected in his field and has received many awards. Jim Jones is now the rave on the media. People all across the world are talking about Jim Jones. Isn't that the perfect opportunity to include what Jim Jones and doctors are saying, for it to be shared? It surely is. A tweet or Facebook post will surely be shared more times by you referencing Jim Jones and the doctor than if you neglect to include the information.

22.   Have you shared your content more than once?
You should share it more than once so that your users will see it. Be mindful that your tweet or other sharing avenue has to compete with tweets and posts from people commenting on the same topic. You have to ensure that your content is visible.

23.   Do you need to create new content all the time?
No. What you can do is rework your content. This means that you create content in one format and then use the same information in other forms. For example, your topic is on gardening and you wrote an article about it. You can use the same topic but make it more interactive by doing a video of you

or a friend gardening and showing exactly how to do certain things. Perhaps you have pictures of how dilapidated your yard once looked compared to how it looks now. You can feature a photo gallery to highlight what you've implemented and showcase how your flowers are now blooming. It is the same information, but you have used various formats. Moreover, this allows the same content to be digested by people who have different preferences. Individuals who prefer reading will appreciate your post. People more inclined to visuals will prefer the pictures and videos. Those who prefer more interaction will prefer the video. All you have to do is be creative with how you rework your content.

24. How often should you publish fresh content?
It depends on the business you are in. Ideally twice a week can suffice. If you post more often, that is remarkable too. However, it is better to have value and quality rather than quantity. If you do post every day, ensure that your content has substance to it. Do not post just because everyone is doing it. Other people's goals will be quite different from yours.

25. Do you really need an editorial calendar?
I highlighted this before, and if you are just starting your business perhaps you may wonder if it applies to you or a big company only. Everything is dependent on your strategy. An editorial calendar is a resource that will keep you more organized and focused on your goals. Do not overlook its importance.

26. What is evergreen content?

Evergreen refers to plants that retain green leaves no matter what the season. Evergreen content is information that stays relevant and fresh despite what is happening. Evergreen content means that long after you have posted your content, it remains important. It does not include the latest trends and fashionable clothing designs, articles on pop culture, articles about the season as they would only be relevant at a particular season, articles about what is happening in the news, and reports on statistics and data.

Evergreen formats include tips, lists, "how to" instructions, and videos. Just because you use these formats doesn't mean that your content will automatically be classed as evergreen. For example, if you do a video highlighting tips on how decorate your home at Christmas, the content is seasonal. However, if you create a video with the topic, "Tips to de-clutter your home," that is a topic that can be discussed all year round.

27.   Is short content or long content better?
Remember we spoke about the length of the paragraphs on your blog post. However, depending on other forms of content, only you can decide what is best for your audience. For example, if you offer ebooks and PDFs, you may prefer to have brief information or you may decide to have a lot of information. It all depends on your audience. You can provide the various options on your website and see what your audience prefers.

28.   What types of content are more successful?

Vary your content. You will not know what is better for your business and your audience unless you test the market. For example, an expert in the industry may say webinars are better but that data may be dependent on what works for that particular expert in his specific industry. Perhaps from the data analytics of the company, their audience was more appreciative of webinars. However, it may not be the same for your audience. The only way to know what is best for you is to offer various content and after analyzing your data, you will know what is best for you.

29.   What tone should you use?
You should use the tone that your audience prefers and what will enhance your brand. If your website is about relationships, a formal tone will not be appropriate. The topics discussed in Chapter 3 will assist you.

30.   Where can I get inspiration for content?
Inspiration can be found on blogs that you enjoy reading. What are your competitors posting? You can approach it from the same and also a different angle. Engage in brainstorming more often. Engage your customers and customer support team. Refer to websites that you like. You can also get inspiration from the comments on your posts.

31.   How do I know what my audience values?
Ensure that you have a format for your audience to comment and continue the dialogue. With the email addresses which you have collected, you can send out questionnaires requesting

that they select the topics they want to know more about. Furthermore, you can also conduct a poll on your website.

32. Do you really need to hire experienced writers when others can create valuable content, too?
You cannot substitute experience with anything else. You are competing with other brands—not just in your locale, but globally. Think long-term instead of short-term. You will receive what you have paid for. If you want quality, hire those who will give you better quality than what others are offering.

33. If someone asks you to define your content, what should you say?
Your content should be mission-driven. What is your mission? Once you can talk about your mission, then you will know how best to define your content.

34. Should you ask other people to use their platform to share your content?
Yes, you should do so. Know who you will link with to ensure that your content is appropriate. When you have published your post, you can email other sites and ask them to share on their social platforms, too.

35. How important is using current events?
Though you may use evergreen topics, depending on your subject, you will need to identify trends and include them in your content. One sure way to increase traffic is to have content about a topic that is trending. For example, if your blog caters

to sports yet you failed to mention anything about the Olympics, that is one huge error.

36.   How significant are keywords?

Though you are writing for an audience, you should also be mindful that keywords help you to improve your ranking. Do not overlook them. Using the example above, with billions of people keying in the word Olympics 2016 in the search engines, many of the sites who have included that keyword have seen an improvement in traffic.

37.   Is guest blogging necessary?

Guest blogging, though it is not mandatory, is a vital marketing strategy that you should consider. Content is content whether it appears on your website or someone else's website. The same rules apply. If you invite someone to blog on your website, ensure that the content has value and vice versa.

38.   Should you outsource or handle content production in-house?

It depends on your resources and time. That is why you have to strategize and plan properly. You may have the capabilities to create content, but what other work-related and personal matters do you have on your calendar? Be realistic. If you know that you will not be able to create quality work, then hire someone or a team to do so.

39.   What is a common mistake?

Writing content that sounds like it was penned by a showy salesman is a very common mistake to make. That is why it is important to focus on your objectives and plan properly before you start writing. It is not about you, but your audience. A sales pitch will not be deemed as valuable by your audience.

40.   How can you measure the success of your efforts?
One method to measure your success is by the number of conversions produced. However, do not look at your present data and think that it is a one-time process. If you posted information and your data shows that 800 people read your post but only 3 bought the item, do not be disappointed. Content marketing is a relationship. You have to keep producing content, not stop when you have just begun. A visitor may read the blog and only after reading several posts weeks later, decide to buy your product. Therefore, give your marketing efforts time, for surely they will pay off and you will reap the benefits.

Chapter 6

Case Studies & Strategies

Huffington Post

The Huffington Post was launched in 2005 and provides the public with news ranging from politics to technology and entertainment and women's interests. In 2012, out of the 15 most popular political sites, it was ranked as #1 by ebizMBA Rank. Moreover, that same year it obtained a Pulitzer Prize.

One of the co-founders, Arianna Huffington, who was born in Greece, ran as an independent candidate for governor in the California recall election in 2003. She did not win, but six years later, in 2009, she was referred to as one of the Most Influential Women in Media. Huffington Post's other co-founders are Ken Lerer and Jonah Peretti.

In 2011, AOL, America Online, acquired the Huffington Post and Arianna became the President and Editor-in-Chief. In

August 2016, she announced that she was leaving her position at the Post, moving on and starting her own company which would focus on wellness.

There are local editions and international editions. The local version was first launched in Chicago in 2007. Thereafter, one was launched in New York followed by Denver, Los Angeles, San Francisco, Detroit, Miami, and Hawaii. There are international editions in various countries, also.

Today the Post is a dominant online news source. It was first a political blog, but now provides readers with a variety of topics such as college life, technology, world news, living, business, and entertainment. The key is the people who are producing their content.

If Huffington Post's content was boring and offered little value, they would not have become a giant in the industry today. They have more than 3,000 contributing bloggers. These contributors include celebrities, academics, and politicians.

Since they started years ago, technology has surely changed, but they have kept abreast and adjusted accordingly.

Last year Huffington Post implemented videos, demonstrating how to make certain dishes to their Facebook fans in 60 seconds or less. For people who are too busy, this simple and time saving technique really appealed to them. This may not seem like a big deal, but Huffington Post was established before Facebook. Adam Denenberg, the Vice President of

Engineering, has expressed in several interviews that his goal was to ensure that the online news source was ready for the influx of users as individuals were accessing content from their mobile devices more than their desktop computers. He focused on a modernized platform to adapt to the change in technology.

He had to ensure that the platform could handle the amount of traffic. Moreover, he had to choose the right software to maximize productivity for their editors. They have the appropriate software where editors from different locations can log on and edit the work without emailing back and forth or using a third-party system.

Lessons

Choose the people who will produce your content very carefully. Huffington Post's bloggers are experts in their respective fields. Just because you are just starting out doesn't mean that you should hire anyone you can find or those whose rates are the cheapest. You need remarkable content. What you do today will reflect on how well you maintain your position in the future.

Ensure that your platform can handle the traffic when it arrives. Moreover, determine how you will interact with your content creation team. Rather than emailing back and forth, you can use a platform where anyone can log on and review or edit a document to save time. Though you need the right editors and writers, they must be also be versed in technology. Can you imagine if you used an editor who insisted on faxing certain information to you rather then emailing? Thus, when scouting for members of your team, consider also how individuals will increase productivity.

Birchbox

Birchbox is based in New York and was launched in 2010 by two graduates from Harvard Business School. It is an online subscription service where subscribers receive samples of makeup and beauty products.

When Birchbox first started, they had 600 subscribers. Now there are over one million subscribers and almost 1000 brand partners. They rely on surveys to garner information about the subscribers.

The company has videos on personal grooming. Very frequently subscribers can access grooming videos for both men and women. It is one thing to read about grooming, but Birchbox has taken it to another level by capitalizing on visuals. The company values its customers by showing them how to look their best. Today they are in more than five countries.

Lessons

Mutual benefit is a key component when strategizing. The company's model is based on sending other companies' products to consumers. If you receive free products and try it and realize how awesome it is, won't you continue using it? Of course you will. This opens up avenue for the manufacturers of the products. Additionally, Birchbox also provides the content about the product. This is a win situation for the manufacturer, in exchange for sending free samples. Consumers can also give their reviews about a product on Birchbox's website.

Content marketing is about interacting with your consumers. Remember, it is about the customers.

Home Depot
The objective of the founders of the Home Depot which started in 1978 was to build superstores that were dedicated to home improvement. The content they provide helps consumers in their everyday lives. For example, they share content on how to save energy or tips on selecting certain items for the holidays such as Christmas trees.

Additionally, the company has YouTube videos with information about home improvements. They not only tell you, but also show you what to do. On Twitter, they also continue with the discussion about decorating and repairs.

The Apron is the name of Home Depot's blog. Their in-store employees add content to the blog. This is an innovative form of content generation, and it also saved the company money by using associates who have the knowledge to communicate what they know to a wider audience. The company will know who is best to write the content, but it adds a bit of personal touch.

Lesson
Your content can answer questions that consumers have. Do not just think short-term but also long-term. Consumers will

have questions and concerns about the upcoming holidays. You do not have to wait until consumers email a question. In our previous illustration, we used the example of someone who has a health blog. You do not have to wait until someone inquires if you have any recipes to share with diabetics. You can think ahead and have information for your users. If your competitor offers the same health topics but also provides recipes, tips, and more information, the audience will gravitate to your competitor's website.

Additionally, using associates to add to content is one way of cementing Home Depot's authority and credibility in the business. An associate who has hands-on experience, who customers know, as opposed to someone who is doing research behind the scenes, adds a personal touch.

The videos help to bridge the gap between the business and consumers. No one is in designer suits talking about home products. Customers see people who look like them who want the best for their money. They can relate to what is being said.

When creating videos, make sure that your attire correlates to your product and overall brand.

Alcatel-Lucent
Alcatel and Lucent Technologies was founded 1872 and 1870 respectively. They produce hardware, software, and telecommunications services. In 2006 they merged and in 2016 the company was acquired by Nokia.

Before being acquired by Nokia, the company launched "The New Guy" campaign. It was a series of sitcom-style videos focusing on customers' problems and thereafter they provided engaging ebooks giving solutions and capturing the consumers' attention. The e-books contained a question and answer format. The sitcom series obtained 600,000 views. This creative campaign was the company's most viewed promotion.

The videos and the e-books had none of the technical jargon that often overwhelms consumers.

Lessons
Keep your messages simple. Do not use language that frustrates your consumers. Instances where you have to use technical or scientific explanation, ensure that it is written in such a way that your audience understands.
This is a wonderful example of how the company used humor to captivate its audience. The videos and e-books were educational, but the injection of humor kept people entertained.

Strategies to implement

Have a support group
Invite a group to support and interact with your content. For example, if your blog is about beauty products and you know that there is a group of makeup artists and hairdressers in your area who meet regularly to give free demonstrations, tell them about your blog post.

If you are new to social media, this will greatly assist you and encourage you on this part of the journey.

Include images in your Tweets.
Use images to garner more attention. However, make sure that your image complements your content and it is a high-quality image.

Let us assume that you tweeted, "Guest blogger and Pastry Chef Molly shares tips on how to make chocolate croissants." With so many people tweeting, the topic may not be seen by your followers, or if they see it they may not be compelled to click on the link. However, if you have a photo showing delicious chocolate croissants, the imagery will cause people to click the link. They may not even read the entire headline, but the image is so appealing that they could not resist clicking on the link.

Make sure that the image you have chosen is not blurry. Also, check for background details. Regardless of which forum you are posting, this should not be overlooked. You may have a computer screensaver that says "I Hate Facebook," yet in your eagerness to show the chocolate croissants to the world you took a picture of them on a platter, forgetting that your computer screen is in the backdrop. Then you post on Facebook. Viewers looking at the picture will surely have lots to think and talk about, and it won't just be about the recipe for the croissants or how great they look. Their focus will be on what is on your computer screen.

Reserve the name you wish to use on various platforms.
You do not have to wait until you are ready to reserve a name. If you are still strategizing, you can sign up and save the name of your brand for future use. For example, if you are conceptualizing your website thebestfans.com, feel free to sign up for the "The Best Fans" on Twitter and Facebook and other popular platforms. That way if someone wants to steal your idea, you do not have to worry because you already own the name.

Moreover, though you may like a particular name, ensure that you conduct research first to determine if the name you have chosen is suitable for your business. You may be creative with a name but if the public has difficulty remembering the name or how to spell it, it may not be as creative as you think.

Schedule when you will check your accounts.
You have worked too much to simply ignore the feedback on the various platforms. You may wait with your phone in your hand, or at your computer, assessing every comment, every like, every share, every reply to the comment, and check to see how many people saw your posts with the data that Facebook provides. That is time you could have spent working on your next strategy or writing your next blog post. Instead, set a time to check your posts. How often you wish to do so is entirely up to you.

Additionally, set your schedule so that you don't forget about your accounts. Do not post and then check back two weeks later.

Let you team promote your posts.
If you have a team, let them share your content. If you do not have a team, ask your friends and family to share your posts.

Share your content many times.
Sharing your content does not mean that you post your blog post, then share on Google Plus if you use that platform, then share on LinkedIn, then follow through with Facebook and Twitter. Share on every platform more than once. Plan a schedule.

Neither does this mean that you share on Facebook every 5 minutes. You can post on Facebook the next day or several days later. It depends on your traffic. If you have 2 people on your Facebook page, you will not have the need to post as frequently as if you have 200,000 followers.

Reply to individuals
If someone contacts you, try your best to respond in a timely manner. If you wrote about Easter discounts and someone asks a question, do not wait until it is summer to reply. By then you have already lost a customer.

Genuinely care about your readers and do all that you can to make their experience worthwhile.

Conclusion

Thank you again for purchasing this book!

Content marketing is more than writing an awesome article. You have to strategize and take the time to analyze your data, observe social trends, monitor your social media platforms, and measure your performance. You have to assess what is working specifically for you and what is hindering your business growth.

Every platform that you use to distribute your content is not static. There are always dynamic changes. Whether it is blogging, using Facebook and Twitter, making videos, or emailing newsletters, you have to integrate the entire process to maximize your results.

Content marketing is not about you, but about your audience. Therefore, you have to adjust your marketing strategy because the behavior of people has changed. Consumers want information with more frequency than before, due to the advancement of technology. They want to gain more knowledge before they are influenced to buy, rather than have someone constantly imploring them to buy. Content marketing is about understanding the needs of your audience and helping them to make an informed decision.

I do hope that this book has offered a deeper insight on the steps you need to take to dominate your field.

Finally, if you enjoyed this book, then I'd like to ask you for a favor, would you be kind enough to leave a review for this book on Amazon? It'd be greatly appreciated!

Thank you and good luck!

Free Marketing Blueprint

Marketing can be a complex subject and even after years of experience the same principles still apply.

Give yourself a head start! Grab your free copy of The Marketing Blueprint to help you understand what you need to succeed

To grab your copy of The Marketing Blue Print visit
http://www.mrmarketinghero.com/freebook

Other Books by Eric J Scott

Content Marketing
Strategies To Capture And Engage Your Audience, While Quickly Building Authority

Content Marketing:
Tips And Tricks To Increase Credibility

Email Marketing:
A Beginner's Guide To Dominating The Market

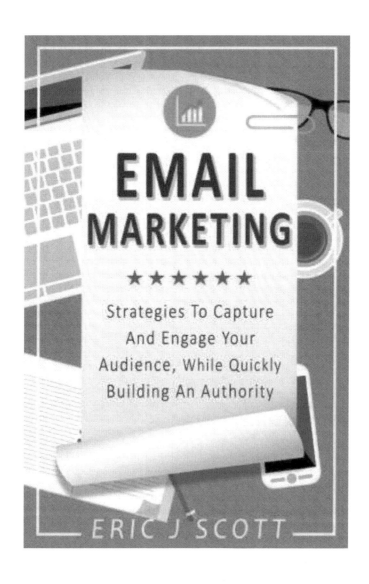

Email Marketing:
Strategies To Capture And Engage Your Audience, While Quickly Building Authority

Email Marketing:
Tips And Tricks To Increase Credibility

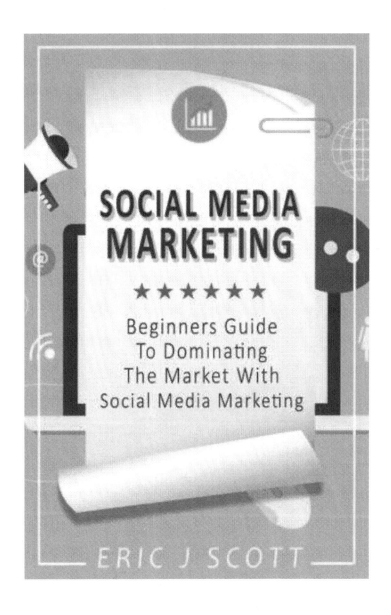

Social Media Marketing
A Beginner's Guide To Dominating The Market

Social Media Marketing:
Strategies To Capture And Engage Your Audience, While Quickly Building Authority

Social Media Marketing:
Tips And Tricks To Increase Credibility

Made in the USA
Lexington, KY
11 April 2017